Benjamin Britten

The World of the Spirit

for soprano, alto, tenor and baritone soloists,
1 or 2 speakers, SATB choir and orchestra

Text compiled by R. Ellis Roberts

Vocal Score

CHESTER MUSIC

CH81587

Head office:
14–15, Berners Street,
London W1T 3LJ
England

Tel +44 (0)20 7612 7400
Fax +44 (0)20 7612 7549

Sales and hire:
Music Sales Distribution Centre,
Newmarket Road,
Bury St Edmunds,
Suffolk IP33 3YB
England

Tel +44 (0)1284 702600
Fax +44 (0)1284 768301

www.musicsalesclassical.com

Full score and orchestral parts are available for hire from the publisher.

Printed in Great Britain

CONTENTS

ORCHESTRATION

2 flutes	2 trumpets in C	percussion (1)	harp
2 oboes	3 trombones	suspended cymbal	organ
2 clarinets in B♭	tuba	clashed cymbals	strings
2 bassoons	timpani	gong	
4 horns in F		side drum	
		bass drum	
		tambourine	

The first performance of this concert version was given on 27 June 1998 in the Snape Maltings Concert Hall as part of the Aldeburgh Festival, by Janice Watson (soprano), Catherine Wyn-Rogers (mezzo-soprano), Timothy Robinson (tenor), Neal Davies (baritone), and David Evans (speaker), with the Joyful Company of Singers and the City of London Sinfonia, conducted by Steuart Bedford.

The World of the Spirit has been recorded by Chandos on CHAN 9487, by Susan Chilcott (soprano), Pamela Helen Stephen (mezzo-soprano), Martyn Hill (tenor), Stephen Varcoe (baritone), and Hannah Gordon and Cormac Rigby (speakers), with the Britten Singers and the BBC Philharmonic, conducted by Richard Hickox.

Full score and orchestral parts are available from the publisher's hire library.
The full score is also on sale, order number CH76527.

Duration: 42 minutes

Prefatory Note

In May 1938 Britten took time off from writing his Piano Concerto to compose *The World of the Spirit*, the second of his religious 'cantatas' specifically conceived for BBC radio, the sung and spoken texts of which were assembled by R. Ellis Roberts. The success of Britten's and Roberts's earlier radio collaboration, *The Company of Heaven* (1937), a meditation in words and music on the subject of angels, had led to a commission for another work of the same genre. *The World of the Spirit* was first broadcast on 5 June 1938, with Sophie Wyss (soprano), who had been the soloist in the first performances of *Our Hunting Fathers* (1936) and *On This Island* (1937), Anne Wood (alto), Emlyn Bebb (tenor) and Victor Harding (bass), and the BBC Singers and Orchestra conducted by Trevor Harvey. The spoken texts were read by Felix Aylmer, Leo Genn and Robert Speaight. The BBC rebroadcast the feature in 1939, after which *The World of the Spirit* remained unheard until its revival in 1995, as part of a BBC Radio 3 series documenting Britten's music for radio.

There are perhaps two important aspects of *The World of the Spirit* that demand particular attention. First, the exceptional 'mix' of styles, genres and forms that characterises Britten's response to his texts, both sung and spoken. If for no other reason, we must take account of this music because it reveals the twenty-four-year-old composer's prodigious versatility and his mastery of a wide range of compositional techniques; while every so often there is an inspiration that reveals the unmistakable musical personality with which we are now familiar.

The second and more significant aspect is tied in with the heterogeneous profile of the first. It was surely the very diversity of the texts – chosen from a wide variety of sources – that challenged the young composer to provide a sequence of music that was in itself *anthological* in character, e.g. plainsong, chorale, orchestral song, oratorio and cantata, Bach-like arioso, a chorus 'number' (the barcarolle), etc., etc. However, behind the diversity of texts and music there is a unity of theme and purpose. We do not know precisely how the texts came to be chosen, though they must have been the subject of discussion between Britten and Roberts. But it can certainly have been no accident that so many of them, whether they have their origins in the Bible, Quaker philosophy, English poetry, or *reportage* of and from historico-political events (the 1914-18 war, the Irish 'troubles'), reflect preoccupations that were to remain the composer's throughout his life: abhorrence of war, violence and intolerance, and the affirming of peace, justice and reconciliation. In short, *The World of the Spirit* was the first step along the road that was eventually to lead to *War Requiem* in 1962 and *Voices for Today*, commissioned for the twentieth anniversary of the United Nations in 1965.

The title of the work finds its musical fulfilment in the extended setting of *Veni Creator Spiritus*, the ancient plainsong for Whitsuntide that both opens the work and brings it to its close. In the final number of the Epilogue, the three choral verses of the plainsong, each gaining in intensity, dissolve in a radiant coda for soprano and strings.

Donald Mitchell and Philip Reed

Editor's Note

In the preparation of this Concert Version of *The World of the Spirit* I have made allowance for the omission of certain of the spoken texts and in some of them have introduced minor revisions, clarifications, and abridgements. Likewise, the Concert Version allows for a reduction in the number of speakers, as compared with the full version, which in the main conforms, we believe, with the programme as it was first heard in 1938. (No sound document of that event remains.) None of the revisions affects the music, which is identical in both performing versions, full or concert.

It will be noticed that in the last bar of virtually each musical number preceding a spoken text Britten includes a fermata. It might well have been his intention that the speaker should begin the text before the sustained chord itself is relinquished.

I would like to thank Paul Kildea and Julian Elloway for their valuable editorial assistance.

Donald Mitchell

The World of the Spirit

Text compiled by
R. Ellis Roberts

BENJAMIN BRITTEN
(1913–1976)

PART I – Prologue

1 Prelude

2 O Thou that movest all

8
mf
flo - wer, Mys - te - rious aim of soul and heart; O
flo - wer, Mys - te - rious aim of soul_ and_ heart; O
flo - wer, Mys - te - rious aim_ of soul and heart; O
flo - wer, Mys - te - rious aim of soul and heart; O
11
f
Life, O Love, how un - di - vi - ded Thou brood-est o'er this world of
Life, O Love, how un - di - vi - ded Thou brood-est o'er this world of_
Life, O Love, how un - di - vi - ded Thou brood-est o'er this world of_
Life, O Love, how un - di - vi - ded Thou brood-est o'er this world of
mf

15 ④ rall.

p *pp*

Thine, Ob - scure and strange, yet sure - ly gui - - -

18 più lento

ppp

- - ded To reach a dis - tant_ end di - vine!

*

SPEAKER 1 The Comforter, which is the Holy Spirit, . . . he shall guide you into all truth.

SPEAKER 2 I assert, for myself, . . . I look *through* it, not with it.

SPEAKER 1 I have learned To look on nature, . . . And rolls through all things.

** optional cut*

3 The sun, the moon, the stars

13
6
the hills,
and the
plains—
8va
loco
sim.
mf
17
mf
Are
not
these,
O
Soul,
the
Vi - sion of
him
who
mf
cresc.
8va
21
ff
p
reigns?
ff
p
8va
ff
mf
dim.

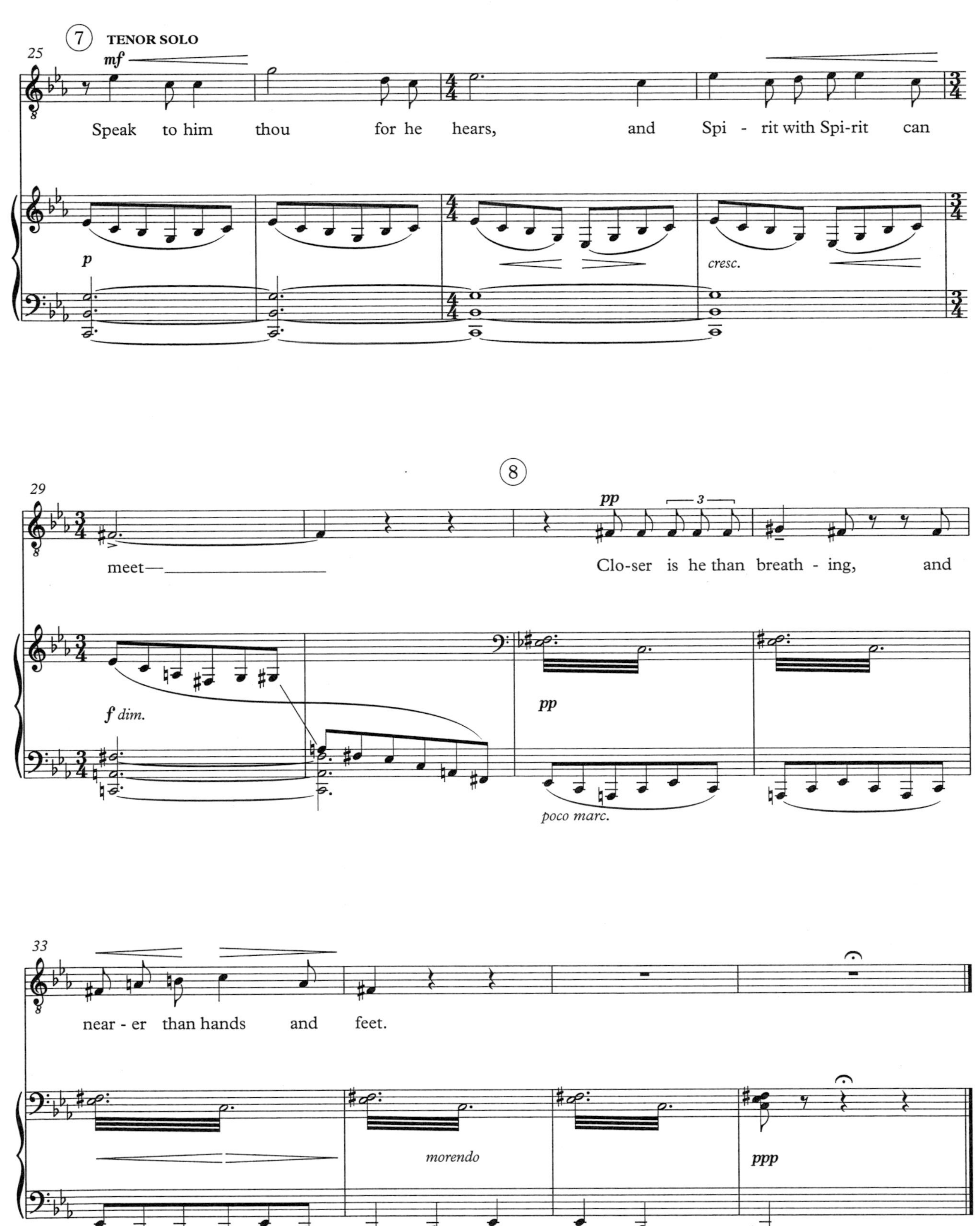

SPEAKER 2 And, behold, the Lord passed by, . . . after the fire a still small voice.

4a This is my commandment

Lento

TENOR SOLO

pp sotto voce

This_ is my com-mand-ment, That ye love one an-o-ther,_ e-ven as I have loved you.

SOPRANO

ALTO

SOLO OCTET

TENOR

BASS

Lento

pp

6

9

SOPRANO: *pp sotto voce*

If ye love me, keep my com-mand-ments. And I will pray the Fa - ther,_ and he shall give you an-o-ther

ALTO: *pp sotto voce*

If ye love me, keep my com-mand-ments. And I will pray the Fa - ther,_ and he shall give you an-o-ther

TENOR: *pp sotto voce*

If ye love me, keep my com-mand-ments. And I will pray the Fa - ther,_ and he shall give you an-o-ther

BASS: *pp sotto voce*

If ye love me, keep my com-mand-ments. And I will pray the Fa - ther,_ and he shall give you an-o-ther

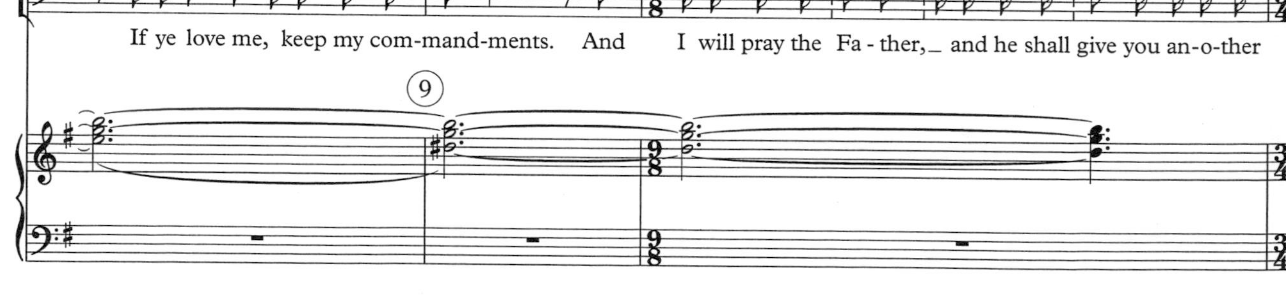

9
pp
Com-fort-er, that he may a-bide with you for ev - er; E - ven the Spi-rit of
Com-fort-er, that he may a-bide with you for ev - er; E - ven the Spi-rit of
Com-fort-er, that he may a-bide with you for ev - er; E - ven the Spi-rit of
Com-fort-er, that he may a-bide with you for ev - er; E - ven the Spi-rit of
13
10
p cresc.
truth; whom the world can-not re-ceive, be-cause it se-eth him not, nei-ther know-eth him: but
truth; whom the world can-not re-ceive, be-cause it se-eth him not, nei-ther know-eth him: but
truth; whom the world can-not re-ceive, be-cause it se-eth him not, nei-ther know-eth him: but
truth; whom the world can-not re-ceive, be-cause it se-eth him not, nei-ther know-eth him: but

17
rall.
ye know him; for he dwell-eth with you, and shall be in you, and shall be
ye know him; for he dwell-eth with you, and shall be in you, and shall be
ye know him; for he dwell-eth with you, and shall be in you, and shall be
ye know him; for he dwell-eth with you, and shall be in you, and shall be
rall.
8va
p cresc.

4b With wide-embracing love

Andante lento

20

SOPRANO SOLO *p* *espress.*

With wide - em - bra - cing love Thy spi - rit a - ni-mates

ALTO SOLO *p* *espress.*

With wide - em - bra - cing love Thy spi - rit a - ni-mates

pp

in you.

pp

in you.

pp

in you.

pp

in you.

Andante lento

8va

f

pp

pp ma sempre pesante

8va

24
e - ter - nal years, Per - vades and broods a - bove,
e - ter - nal years, Per - vades and broods a - bove,
8va
loco
11
28
mf
dim.
Chan - ges, sus - tains, dis - solves, cre - ates, dis - solves, cre - ates and rears.
mf
dim.
Chan - ges, sus - tains, dis - solves, cre - ates, dis - solves, cre - ates and rears.
S.
TUTTI mf
Though
A.
TUTTI mf
Though
T.
TUTTI mf
Though
B.
TUTTI mf
Though
11
mf espress.
p
8va

12
32
earth and man were gone, And suns and u-ni-vers-es
earth and man were gone, And suns and u-ni-vers-es
earth and man were gone, And suns and u-ni-vers-es
earth and man were gone, And suns and u-ni-vers-es
12
(col 8ve)
mf espress.
sempre pesante
8va
35
espress.
ceased to be, And thou wert left a-lone,
espress.
ceased to be, And thou wert left a-lone,
espress.
ceased to be, And thou wert left a-lone,
espress.
ceased to be, And thou wert left a-lone,
cresc.
solo cello
f
8va

39
f espress.
Ev - 'ry ex - ist - ence would ex - ist, ev - 'ry ex - ist - ence
f espress.
Ev - 'ry ex - ist - ence would ex - ist, ev - 'ry ex - ist - ence
f espress.
Ev - 'ry ex - ist - ence would ex - ist, ev - 'ry ex - ist - ence
f espress.
Ev - 'ry ex - ist - ence would ex - ist, ev - 'ry ex - ist - ence
espress.
poco dim.
8va
42
13
pp
would ex - ist in thee.
pp
would ex - ist in thee.
pp
would ex - ist in thee.
pp
would ex - ist in thee.
13
espress.
pp
8va
loco
poco marc.

45
pp
pp

48
pp
ppp

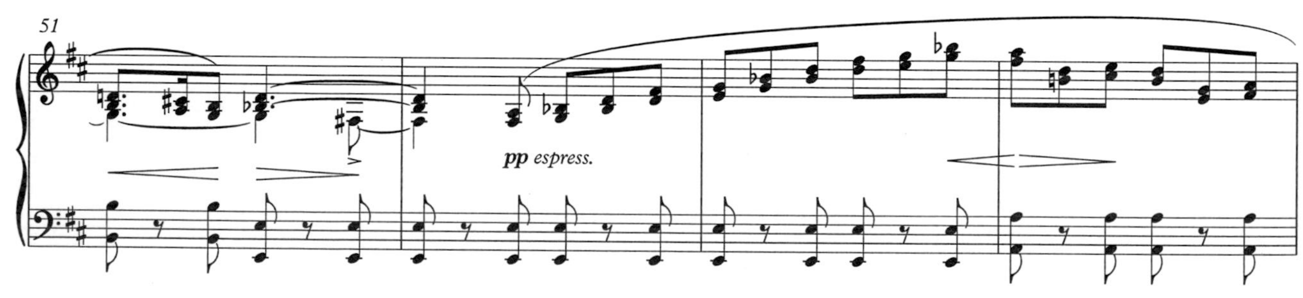
51
pp espress.

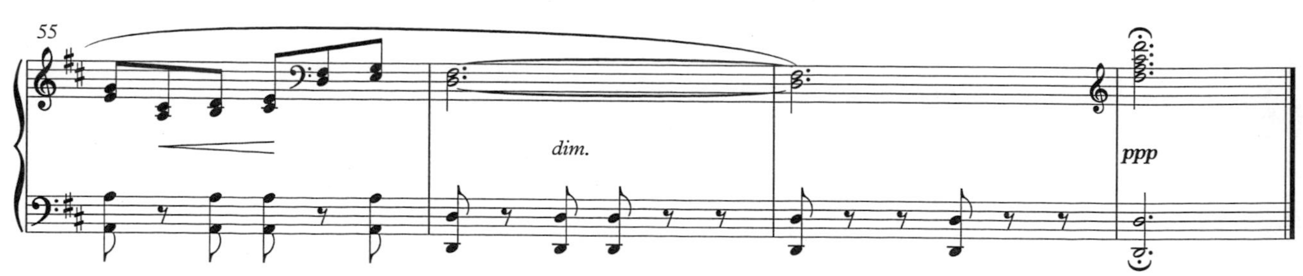
55
dim.
ppp

PART II – The fruits of the Spirit

SPEAKER 2 Lord make me see thy glory . . . Through will, thro' senses, purging what is base!

5 O Life, O Love, now undivided

13
15
pp sost.
pp
S.
B.
T.
B.
We know Thee in the doubt and ter - ror That reels be-fore the
8va
ppp
pp
18
p
world we see; We knew Thee in the faiths of er - ror: We

22
16
mf
know Thee most who most are free. This phan-tom of the world a-round
know Thee most who most are free. This phan-tom of the world a-round
know Thee most who most are free. This phan-tom of the world a-round
know Thee most who most are free. This phan-tom of the world a-round
16
mf
26
f
p
Thee Is vast, di - vine, but not the whole: We wor-ship Thee, and
Thee Is vast, di - vine, but not the whole: We wor-ship Thee, and
Thee Is vast, di - vine, but not the whole: We wor-ship Thee, and
Thee Is vast, di - vine, but not the whole: We wor-ship Thee, and
f
p

31
rall.
pp
più lento
ppp
17
a tempo, largamente
we have found Thee In all that sa - tis - fies the soul!
we have found Thee In all that sa - tis - fies the soul!
we have found Thee In all that sa - tis - fies the soul!
we have found Thee In all that sa - tis - fies the soul!
rall.
più lento
17
a tempo, largamente
pp
36
S. Solo
A. Solo
S.A.
T.B.
pp espress. e cresc.
O
pp espress. e cresc.
f
How shall we serve Thee?
unis. mf
How shall we serve, how shall we own Thee, O
unis. mf
mf
espr.
R.H.
pp

41
f
breath of_ thought!
pp cresc.
How
più f
Breath of Love and Life and Thought?
How shall we praise, who
più f
p
più f
45
pp cresc.
How
f
shall we praise Thee?
cresc.
are_ not_ shown Thee?
How shall we serve, who
cresc.
p
p
p cresc.

49
18
S. Solo
shall we serve Thee?
S.A.
are as nought? Yet, though thy worlds main - tain un - bro - -
T.B.
18
mf
f
53
19
mf espress. e cresc.
A voice
- ken The si - lence of their awe - ful round,
A
mf
19
p

SPEAKER 1 Where the Spirit of the Lord is, . . . they are the sons of God.

6a A voice within our souls

SPEAKER 2 (over chord): The Fruit of the Spirit is love, . . . faith, meekness, temperance.

SPEAKER 1 By their fruits ye shall know them.

6b The fruit of the Spirit is love

SPEAKER 1 One day in November 1682, William Penn . . . This is what Penn said:

SPEAKER 2 'It is not our custom to use hostile weapons . . . all is to be openness, brotherhood, love.'

6c The fruit of the Spirit is faith

Allegro

BASS SOLO

mf 3

The fruit of the Spi - rit is faith, is

mf *cresc.*

7

f espress.

faith, is faith, is faith.

f *dim.* *ppp*

SPEAKER 1 A woman of Canaan cried unto Jesus, saying, . . . And her daughter was made whole from that very hour.

6d The fruit of the Spirit is goodness

6
dim.
pp
good - - ness, is meek - ness,___ is meek - ness.___
espress.
pp
ppp

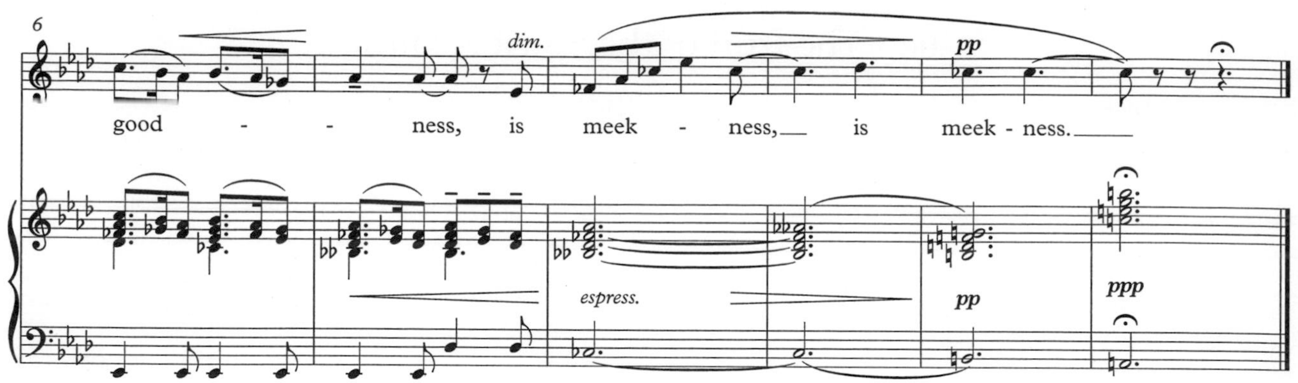

SPEAKER 2 During the First World War, . . . He died moments later.

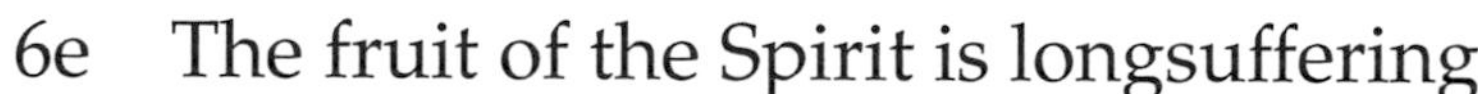

6e The fruit of the Spirit is longsuffering

Comodo
ALTO SOLO
p
The fruit of the Spi - rit is long - suf - fer-ing,
p legato
cresc.

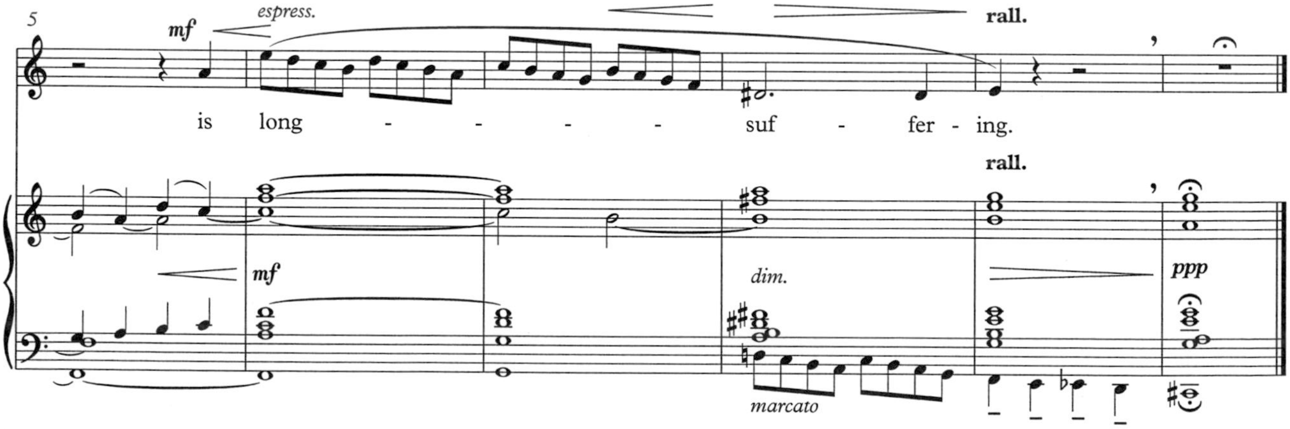

5
mf
espress.
rall.
is long - - - - suf - fer - ing.
rall.
mf
dim.
ppp
marcato

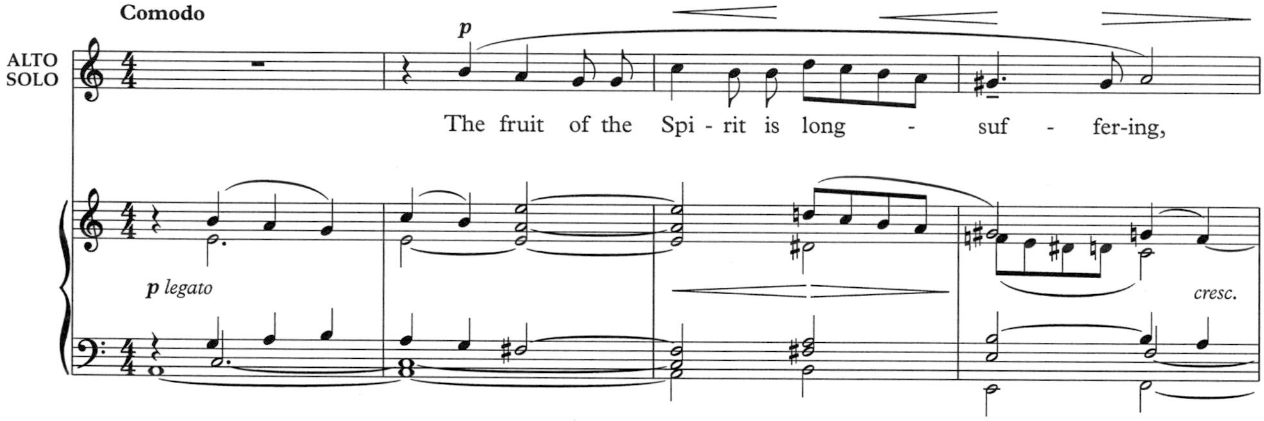

SPEAKER 1 When James Connolly, the Irish Rebel, was under trial . . . that was to bring him to the place of execution.

6f The fruit of the Spirit is joy

SPEAKER 1 St Francis of Assisi once gave this wise advice to a novice:

SPEAKER 2 'My brother, why that sad face? . . . when one is engaged in the service of God.'

SPEAKER 1 No man can make God visible; . . . a flame of fire divine in all things burning.

7 The spirit of the Lord

10
-lu - y'al - le - lu - ya, al - le - lu - ya, al - le - lu - ya! Al - le - lu-ya!
-lu - y'al - le - lu - ya, al - le - lu - ya, al - le - lu - ya! Al - le - lu-ya!
-lu - y'al - le - lu - ya, al - le - lu - ya, al - le - lu - ya! Al - le - lu-ya!
-lu - y'al - le - lu - ya, al - le - lu - ya, al - le - lu - ya! Al - le - lu-ya!
21
16
Al - le - lu - ya, al - le - lu - ya, al - le - lu - ya, al - le - lu - ya, al - le-
Al - le - lu - ya, al - le - lu - ya, al - le - lu - ya, al - le - lu - ya, al - le-
Al - le - lu - ya, al - le - lu - ya, al - le - lu - ya, al - le - lu - ya, al - le-
Al - le - lu - ya, al - le - lu - ya, al - le - lu - ya, al - le - lu - ya, al - le-
21

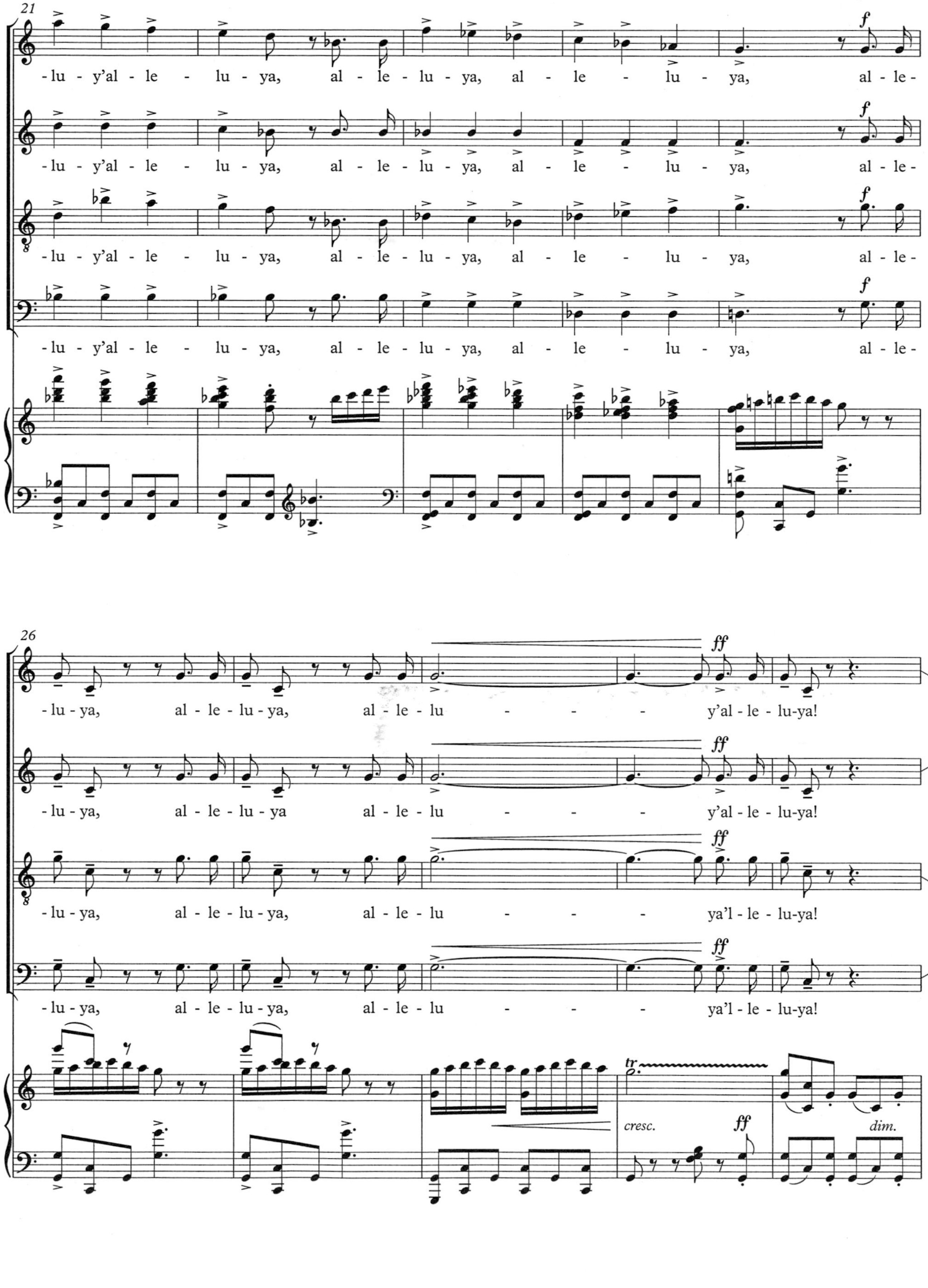

26

ff

- lu - ya, al - le - lu - ya, al - le - lu - - - y'al - le - lu-ya!

ff

- lu - ya, al - le - lu - ya al - le - lu - - - y'al - le - lu-ya!

ff

- lu - ya, al - le - lu - ya, al - le - lu - - - ya'l - le - lu-ya!

ff

- lu - ya, al - le - lu - ya, al - le - lu - - - ya'l - le - lu-ya!

tr

cresc. ff *dim.*

31
22
S.
A.
T.
B.
mf
espress.
O send forth thy spi - rit, and they shall be
mf espress.
sim.
p
36
23
pp
made: Al - le - lu - ya, al - le - lu - ya! And
f
dim.
pp
mf
41
thou shalt re - new the peace of the earth, Al - le-
sim.
cresc.
dim.
f
pp

46
cresc.
-lu - ya, al - le - lu - ya, al - le - lu - ya, al - le -
cresc.
(col 8va)
cresc.
49
mf
-lu - ya, al - le - lu - - - - ya!
mf
p
mf cresc.
sim.
sim.
24
53
ALTO
f
sfp
Al - le - lu - ya, al - le - lu - ya, al - le - lu - - - - ya!
BASS
f
sfp
O send forth thy spi - rit, and they shall be made.
24
10
f
f marc.
sfp

58 SOPRANO SOLO (♩. = 𝅗𝅥)

mp espress.

I will not leave you

TENOR SOLO

mp espress.

I will not leave you

A.

B.

(♩. = 𝅗𝅥)

10

sim.

10

10

sim.

64
- - - le - lu - ya!
- - - le - lu - ya!
10
10
cresc.
67
25
S. Solo
T. Solo
CHORUS
SOPRANO
f
Al - le - lu - ya, al - le - lu - ya, al - le - lu - -
TENOR
f
And thou shalt re - new the peace of the
25
fz
f marc.

71
ALTO SOLO
mp espress.
I will come to
BASS SOLO
mp espress.
I will come to
S.
sfp
- ya!
T.
sfp
earth.
10
sim.
10
10
sfp
pp
sim.
74
A. Solo
you a - gain, and your
B. Solo
you a - gain, and your
10
10
10

77
heart shall be joy - ful.
heart shall be joy - ful.
10
10
26
80
S.
A.
CHORUS
T.
B.
f
Al - le - lu - ya, al - le - lu - ya!
Al - le - lu - ya, al - le - lu - ya!
O
O send forth thy spi - rit.
O send forth thy spi - rit.
Al - le -
26
fz
f marc.

85
27
O send forth thy spi - rit.
send forth thy spi - rit. Al - le - lu
Al - le - lu - ya! Al - le - lu
- lu - ya, al - le - lu - ya! Al - le - lu
fzpp
89 SOPRANO AND ALTO SOLI
mf espress.
I will come to you
TENOR AND BASS SOLI
mf espress.
- ya!
- ya!
- ya!
sempre pp

92
dim.
S.
A.
SOLI
— a - gain, and your heart shall be
T.
B.
dim.
pp
95
28
joy - ful.
pp
S.
Al - le - lu - ya, al - le -
A.
CHORUS
T.
pp
B.
O send forth thy
28
dim.
pp
marc.

99
-lu - ya, al - le - lu - - ya!
pp
Al - le - lu - ya, al - le - lu - ya, al - le - lu - -
pp
O send forth thy spi - rit and they shall be
spi - rit, and they shall be made.
pp marc.
105
pp
Al - le - lu - ya, al - le - lu - ya!
p cresc.
O send forth thy
- ya!
p
O send forth thy spi - rit.
made.
pp
Al - le - lu - ya, al - le - lu - ya!
p
O send forth thy spi - rit.
p cresc.
Al - le - lu - ya, al - le-
pp marc.
p
cresc.
col 8va basso

111
29
mf
spi - rit.
Al - le - lu - ya!
Al - le - lu - ya!
Al - le - lu - ya, al - le - lu - ya, al - le - lu - ya!
Al - le - lu - ya!
O send forth thy spi - rit.
Al - le - lu - ya!
Al - le-
- lu - ya!
Al - le - lu - ya!
Al - le-
mf espress.
mf cresc.
poco a poco cresc.
117
f
Al - le - lu - ya!
Al - le - lu - ya, al - le - lu - ya!
Al - le -
Al - le - lu - ya!
Al - le - lu - ya, al - le - lu - ya!
Al - le -
- lu - ya!
Al - le - lu - ya!
Al - le - lu - ya!
- lu - ya!
Al - le - lu - ya!
Al - le - lu - ya!
(col 8va)
ff
non marc.
side drum

123
30
f
-lu - ya, al - le - lu - ya! Al - le - lu - ya, al - le - lu - ya! Al - - le - - lu -
-lu - ya, al - le - lu - ya! Al - le - lu - ya, al - le - lu - ya! Al - - le - - lu -
Al - le - lu - ya! Al - le - lu - ya, al - le - lu - ya! Al - - le - - lu -
Al - le - lu - ya! Al - le - lu - ya, al - le - lu - ya! Al - - le - - lu -
ff
129
cresc.
- ya! Al - - le - lu - - - ya!
- ya! Al - - le - lu - - - ya!
- ya! Al - - le - lu - - - ya!
- ya! Al - - le - lu - - - ya!
fp cresc.

31
Largamente
136
SOPRANO AND ALTO SOLI
ff
I will come to you a - gain,
ff
TENOR AND BASS SOLI
ff
S.
A.
I will come to you a - gain,
T.
B.
ff
31 Largamente
ff
32
Maestoso
143
fff
and your heart shall be joy - ful.
33
Tempo 1mo
fff
unis. fff
and your heart shall be joy - ful.
unis. fff
32 Maestoso
33 Tempo 1mo
fff

150
S.
A.
ORUS
T.
B.
Al-le - lu - - - ya! Al-le - lu - - -
A-le - lu - - - ya! Al-le - lu - - -
col 8va
157
- ya! Al-le - lu - - - ya!
lunga

PART III - Epilogue

*

SPEAKER 1	Spirit to whom my spirit would reply, . . . O Lord, a sacramental path for thee.
SPEAKER 2	I saw myself as a youth, . . . the face of Christ, a face like all men's faces.

8 O knowing, glorious Spirit!

* *optional cut*

10
- - ing, glo - rious Spi - rit! When Thou shalt re - store trees, beasts, and
cresc.
13
espress.
men, When Thou shalt make all new, new a - gain,
espress.
mf
16
Des - troy - ing on - ly death and pain,
dim.
35
19
pp
Give him a - mongst Thy works a place Who
p cresc.
pp
cresc.

SPEAKER 2 One afternoon I went out . . . I had never looked for him. But he had found me.

9 The world is charged

13
fz
ooze
of
oil
Crushed.
fz
8va
cresc.
ff
17
dim.
f sempre
38
3
21
unis.
f marc.
Why
do
men
then
now
unis.
f marc.
3
3
dim.

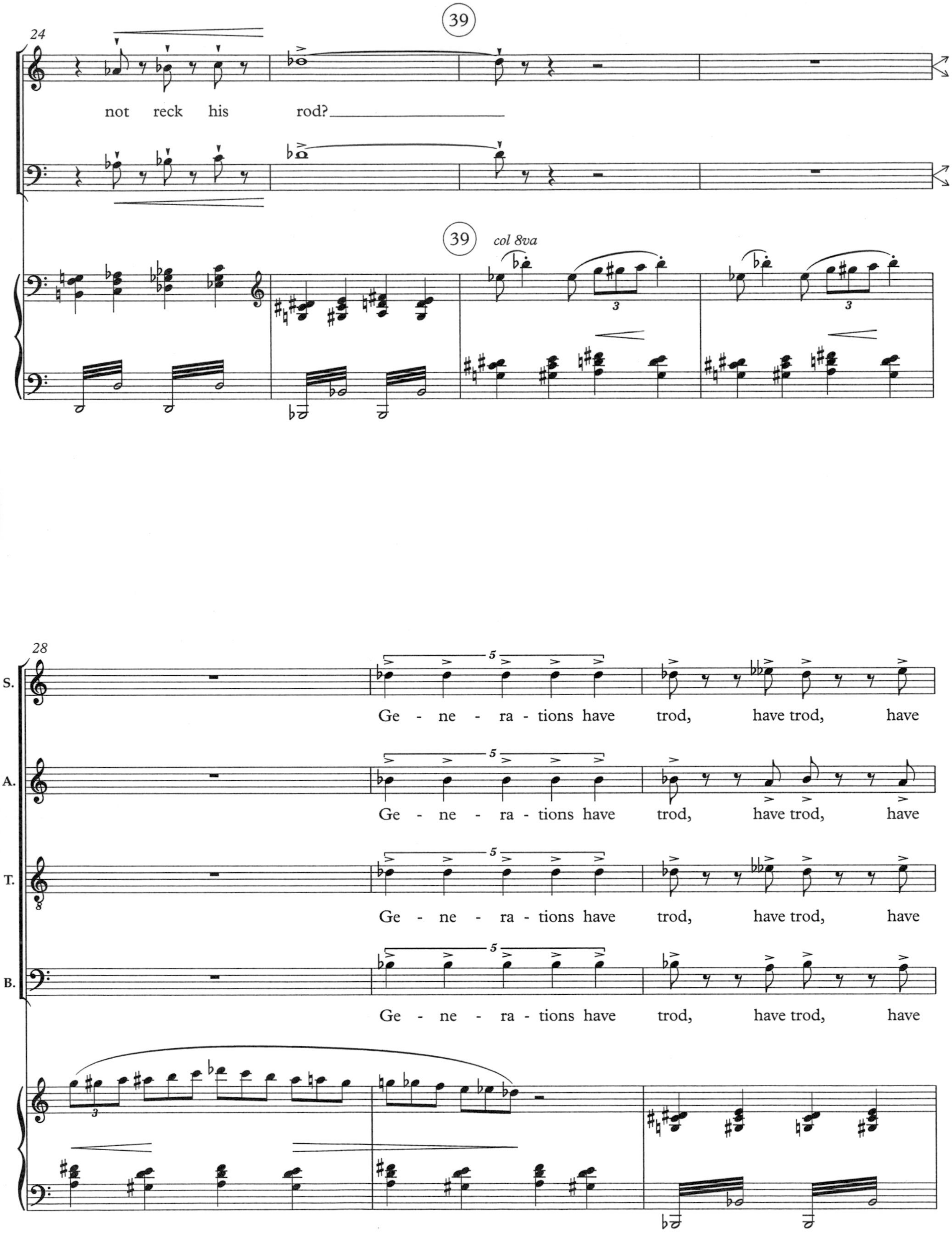

28

S.
Ge - ne - ra - tions have trod, have trod, have

A.
Ge - ne - ra - tions have trod, have trod, have

T.
Ge - ne - ra - tions have trod, have trod, have

B.
Ge - ne - ra - tions have trod, have trod, have

31
40
trod, have trod, have trod;
trod, have trod, have trod;
pp
trod, have trod, have trod, have trod, have trod;
pp
trod, have trod, have trod, have trod, have trod;
40
dim.
mf
p
35
p
And all is seared with
p
And all is seared with
p
And all is seared with
p
And all is seared with

41
38
cresc.
trade; bleared, smeared with toil; And wears man's
cresc.
trade; bleared, smeared with toil; And wears man's
cresc.
trade; bleared, smeared with toil; And wears man's
cresc.
trade; bleared, smeared with toil; And wears man's
41
mf
8va
43
f
ff
smudge and shares man's smell: the
f
ff
smudge and shares man's smell: the
f
ff
smudge and shares man's smell: the
f
ff
smudge and shares man's smell: the

42
47
fz
soil
Is
bare now,
nor can
foot
feel,
be - ing
42
ff
8va
52
fff
shod.

56
SOPRANO SOLO
43
mf
And for
(trem.)
8va
mf
pp
61
all this, na-ture ne-ver is spent; There lives the dear - est fresh-ness
8va
sim.
sim.
67
S. SOLO
deep down things; And though the last lights off the
44
mf
S.
A.
T.
B.
pp
And
8va
pp

72
f
black west went, Oh, morn - -
mf
Oh, morn - -
mf
Oh, morn - -
mf
Oh, morn - -
mf
Oh, morn - -
8va
poco cresc.
mf
45
cresc.
sf dim.
76
3
- ing, at the brown brink east - - ward springs—
sf dim.
- - - - ing springs—
sf dim.
- - - - ing springs—
sf dim.
- - - - ing springs—
sf dim.
- - - - ing springs—
45
8va
cresc.
ff
dim.

80
pp
8va
loco
col 8va
p
85
46
Be - cause the Ho - -
fp
pp poco marc.
solo timp.
solo tpt.
pp sempre

89
- - ly Ghost o - ver the bent World broods
- - ly Ghost o - ver the bent World broods
- - ly Ghost o - ver the bent World broods
- - ly Ghost o - ver the bent World broods
- - ly Ghost o - ver the bent World broods
p col 8va
p
47
93
p
with warm breast and with ah! bright
rf
with warm breast and with ah! bright
with warm breast and with ah! bright
with warm breast and with ah! bright
with warm breast and with ah! bright
47
p
f

SPEAKER 1 God is a Spirit; . . . bears witness unto our spirit, that we are the Children of God.

10 Come, O Creator Spirit, come

16
51
The sign of God's al - might-y power; The Fa - ther's pro - mise, ma - king rich
f
cresc.
22
52
(unis.)
ff con tutta forza
Our sen - ses with thy
With sa-ving truth our earth - ly speech. Our sen - ses with thy
f
mf cresc.
27
53
più f
light in - flame, Our hearts to hea-ven-ly love re - claim; Our bo-dies' poor in -
cresc.

33
S.
A.
T.
B.
ff
sf
5
-firm - i - ty With strength per - pe - tu - al for - ti - fy.
più f
fff
54
Largamente
SPEAKER 2 Where the spirit of the Lord is, there is liberty.
ff espress.
f
mf
p
3
37

rall.
55
SOPRANO SOLO
pp dolciss.
più lento
As many as are led by the spirit of God, they are the sons of God.
O Com - fort - er, that
dim.
pp dolciss.
56
name is thine, Of God most high the gift di - vine; The well of life, the fire of love,
pp
morendo
57
Lento molto
Our souls' a - noint-ing from a - bove.
unis.
ppp
S.A.
A - - - men.
T.B.
unis.
ppp
57
Lento molto
morendo
ppp